Your

As my way of saying thank for buying I put together two amazing free gifts for you.

These gifts are the ultimate bonus upgrade to this book…

The Brain Boosting Recipe Guide

&

The Sleep Hackers Quick Guide

To Download Visit:

www.GoodLivingPublishing.com/Brain

Thanks,

Andy Arnott

Contents

Introduction 4
Memory 2.0 6
Brain Busters 10
   Fatigue 10
   Anxiety, Stress & Depression 10
   Smoking 11
   Nutrition 11
   Thyroid Disorder 12
   Hormones 12
What Improves Memory 13
   Nutrition 13
   Get Organized 14
   Eliminate / Minimize Stress 14
   Exercise 15
   Sleep 15
   Understand Your Attention Span 16
   Use Your Eyes 17
   Aromatherapy 17
   Environmental Clues 18
   Use Your Voice 18
   Breathing 19
   Marital Status 19
Memory Tricks and Tips 21
   Chunking 21
   Association 22
   Acronyms 23

Acrostics	23
Imagery	24
Daily Practices	**27**
Brain Games	27
Concentration	28
Chess	28
Other Puzzles	29
Playing Time	29
Quick List of Tactics for Boosting Your Brain Power	**30**
Conclusion	**33**

Introduction

Interest in brain function and memory continues to grow on a daily basis, be it because of an aging population or increased demands at work or simply to enjoy a better quality of life. It was once believed that memory, as well as IQ, were fixed attributes. You either had a good memory or a bad one.

However, we now know that is not the case.

We now know that you can improve your memory in a variety of ways. They do not require trips to the doctor or a learning lab. In fact many of the ways you can improve your memory do not relate directly to using or training your brain.

To improve your memory and cognitive functioning, you must first have a basic understanding or how the brain and memory work. You do not have to be a neuroscientist. You just need to understand some basic principles.

Once you have the general idea of how the brain works, it is critical to learn about what negatively impacts the brain and memory. This is what the first sections of this book are about and it is all about laying a foundation for your memory enhancement. Once an understanding is achieved, you will learn what improves your brain from a lifestyle perspective. While you may not be able to make dramatic changes to every area of your lifestyle to improve your memory and brain functioning (like quit a high stress job), you will learn ways to help mitigate the elements of your lifestyle that negatively impact the performance of your body's supercomputer.

After lifestyle considerations are addressed, the secondary sections of this book provide a variety of tips, tricks, and daily practices to improve your memory and functioning. Again, the focus of these tools is to be enjoyable, easy to implement, and effective. You do not have to implement all of the suggestions in this book to see improvements to your brain, IQ and memory.

Even one or two tricks can provide a noticeable improvement. The goal is to try the tricks and see what works best for you based on your personal preferences and the reasons for upgrading your brain.

You will see an improvement in your functioning by using the tools and techniques in this book in a matter of hours, not days. In fact, many of the tricks and tips covered can be learned and implemented in minutes.

Much of this book is particularly geared towards improving and upgrading your memory, there is a very specific reason for this. By choosing to focus upon improving your memory first and foremost you will see a huge layover into the level of your cognitive functioning and IQ. The brain is all interconnected and improving one area will flow into improvements in other areas, the most powerful way to do this is to place a large focus on memory improvement.

You might be wondering… can improving your brain power enhance your relationships, your work performance, your earning potential, your ability to learn easily, your overall quality of life and even how you feel about yourself? Yes, it can!

Are you ready to quickly and easily improve your brain, memory and IQ?

Well, there's no better time than right now to learn how your brain and memory work so you can start to change your entire life.

Memory 2.0

Until recently, memory was viewed two ways.

One, it was believed that memory was a fixed commodity. You either had a good memory, a bad memory, or a memory that fell somewhere in between.

It was believed to be similar to other personal traits like hair or eye color. What you had at birth is what you had to work with, period. People understood a good memory may become a bad memory for a variety of reasons, but it was not a common belief that a bad memory could become a better one.

Two, memory was believed to be located in a distinct area of the brain. A popular notion was that memory was like a file cabinet, when recalling something the brain would open up the drawer labelled "memory" and look for the file title with the memory (say "wedding proposal") and read the file. If a person had a bad memory, the thought was that the filing system was in disarray or the file cabinet was damaged causing memories to be lost in the system of the brain.

That was twentieth century thinking.

In the twenty-first century, our knowledge about how the brain works has created a new model for how memory works. We will call this new memory model "Memory 2.0".

Now, doctors and scientist understand that the brain is not simply a mass in the cranium. It is a muscle. Like other muscles in the body, the brain and its memory function can be developed and improved with exercise. In fact, without regular exercise or stimulation the brain atrophies just like other muscles in the body that become weak and shrink without use.

As far as the concept of the memory working like a fixed object, memory 2.0 does not work like a file cabinet. In fact, memory is not a discrete part of the brain at all. While tasks like speech can be traced back to specific areas of the brain, memory is a brain-wide function. A stroke can cause a person to lose all or part of the ability to speak or function in particular ways, but a stroke does not necessarily cause a person's memory to suffer. How is that possible? Well, memory is tied to connections made throughout the brain. The more connections associated with a memory and made within the brain, the better the memory performs, even in situations where specific parts of the brain are damaged. This is one reason that a person who has Alzheimer's disease can have difficulty with some memory processes while maintaining a sharp recollection of distant memories or to those items that have a strong emotional tie. The fact is, to improve your memory you need to simply improve the number and quality of the associations and connections you make with what you aim to remember.

Memory, as a process, is divided into two components: short term memory and long term memory. Even as a memory is being created it is being processed, and meaning is being given.

This is part of survival. Think about what would happen if a caveman had to stop, experience a threat, and then wait to process what it all meant before being able to defend himself. Yes, if we had to stop and think about thinking, the human race would never have survived. This almost instantaneous processing is indeed part of the memory process and it is called sensory memory.

The associations made while in the middle of an experience are connected to previous events and prior knowledge. The transition from sensory memory and perception to processing is part of your short term memory process. Short term memory is like a filter, deciding what is important and what is not, that holds information for a matter of seconds. If you have ever been in a situation when your mind has wandered in class or in a business meeting only to be called on to recollect something the speaker just said, you have used your short term memory storage of stimuli to reply (hopefully, correctly) with what was just covered.

While sensory memory and short term memory quickly decay, a healthy brain has the ability to store unlimited amounts of information indefinitely. This ability is called long term memory, which is what most people generally refer to as "memory". Long term memory uses past experience to inform the current situation and provides a pathway for the brain to remember the event as an association between past and present for future reference and meaning.

Forgetting things, for a healthy person, is the result of one or more problems related to the three Rs: registration, retention, or retrieval. Forgetting due to a problem in registration is because of an issue with how you encoded the information in the first place. When you forget where you put your car keys, you have not really forgotten. Instead, you may have been distracted when you put them down, so your brain did not encode the placement as being important. Similarly, if you always put your keys in the same place, you may not be able to recall the moment you put them down in their proper place because the habitual nature of the act will cause your brain to register the act as not important enough to create a detailed or lasting memory.

Memory problems related to retention are common, especially when reading. When you have to go back and re-read material, this is not simply a reading retention problem; it is a memory retention issue. Your eyes may have covered every word on the page, but you were distracted and the short term memory did not hold the information long enough to let your long term memory process it for future reference.

Retrieval issues stem from a mismatch between the retrieval cues you associated with the material and the encoding of the information you were searching for in your memories. Retrieval problems often happen in instances where you try to remember something like a name or film title but cannot. Then later, the information seems to simply pop into your head. The time between the attempt to recollect information and the actual remembrance of the material is where your brain continued to search for the memory and reconcile the mismatch between retrieval cues and encoded material. That is why it seems beneficial at times to stop trying to remember what you seek. It is like you are looking to unlock the door to your memory with a keypad code. You keep punching in different codes to access the material (retrieval cues) without success, and then after you relax and stop actively thinking about it, you realize the key to the lock was in your pocket the whole time. You remembered the proper retrieval cue (the key), and you got immediate access to your desired memory.

To improve your memory, it does not take a medical degree. By understanding the basic components of how memory works, you can begin to maximize your mental efficiency while beginning to address potential blockages in how you process information in your long term memory. Your memory is directly tied to your overall health and wellbeing, so in addition to understanding how your brain works, it is critical to understand and identify potential problems that can negatively impact your memory.

Brain Busters

The brain is the body's super computer. As a result, the brain can be negatively impacted by a wide range of influences, some of which are easy to recognize and some that are surprising.

While every possible negative influence on memory would take volumes to discuss, the following section covers some of the more widely known hazards to your memory as well as some surprising newly-identified factors.

Fatigue

Fatigue is on the rise as the demands of daily life increase. As people attempt to fit more and more into each day, sleep is often one of the first areas where people cut back. Sleep problems are directly tied to poor performance in both physical and cognitive tests. A lack of sleep impairs physical performance and causes a lack of focus that can contribute to memory problems.

A lack of sleep is not always a lifestyle choice, however. Those who suffer from Chronic Fatigue Syndrome (CFS) have shown decreased functioning on memory tests. In addition to CFS, chronic pain impairs memory and affects a person's ability to work, sleep and function on a daily basis. A study done at the University of Alberta showed that 16 of the 24 participants that had pain for six months or longer showed significant disruption of attention and memory.

Anxiety, Stress & Depression

A 2007 study in the journal *Neurology* in 2007 showed that those who experience negative emotions, such as anxiety, stress and depression, were 40% more likely to develop mild to moderate memory impairment.

Smoking

According to a study in the *Archives of Internal Medicine,* Middle-aged smokers appear to be at an increased risk of having poor memory. The research also showed that long-term ex-smokers were less likely to have cognitive deficits in memory and vocabulary than those who never quit.

Nutrition

Vitamin deficiencies can cause decreased memory function. Specifically, a vitamin B-12 (Cobalamin) deficiency can be accompanied by fatigue and memory impairment. A deficit in amino acids can also negatively influence cognitive recall. Those who are anemic or have lower red blood cell counts can have memory problems due to the fact that red blood cells carry oxygen to the brain that allows for proper functioning. Without adequate iron in the diet the brain can develop a mild case of oxygen deprivation that negatively impacts recall ability.

New research shows excess tofu consumption may increase the risk of memory loss. A study of more than 700 people aged 52-98 who ate tofu at least once a day was performed by Loughborough and Oxford universities. Participants, especially those in their 60s, had an increased risk of memory loss. It has been hypothesized that the Estrogens contained in soy products (including tofu and soy milk) as well as the Estrogens found in plastic containers that include the chemical Bisphenal-A (BPA) are a major contributor to memory concerns.

Excessive carbohydrates, including sugars, have been tied to memory issues related to Alzheimer's and other memory impairments. When blood sugar spikes, the insulin-degrading enzyme in the brain that works overtime removing insulin cannot rid the body of beta-amyloid proteins. These proteins degrade brain function and have been tied to memory loss and Alzheimer's disease.

Thyroid Disorder

Memory loss is a common symptom of an underactive thyroid, according to the Mayo Clinic. Hormones from the thyroid help control a host of bodily functions, ranging from heart rate to mood and memory. People with this treatable condition may exhibit only one symptom, such as memory loss or decreasing mental function.

Hormones

Hormonal fluctuations can cause memory issues. As previously discussed, Estrogens are believed to contribute to memory problems, and women experience fluctuations in both estrogen and iron levels on a monthly basis which can cause temporary memory problems. In addition to the monthly cycle, the University of Illinois at Chicago confirmed a link between hot flashes and poor verbal memory among women in mid-life. The study showed that the more hot flashes a woman had, the worse her ability to remember names and stories became. A surge in the stress hormone cortisol, which usually accompanies a hot flash, was cited as the probable cause.

What Improves Memory

First and foremost, if memory concerns are linked to potential medical conditions, a thorough discussion and exam by a medical professional is the most important step to improving your memory and maintaining your overall health. While the discussion of the negative influences on memory featured both health and lifestyle considerations, this discussion of what can be done to improve your memory will focus on lifestyle choices, though you should consult a doctor prior to implementing dietary changes.

Nutrition

Your brain is a muscle like your heart and other muscles. A well-balanced diet is needed for overall health as well as proper mental function. Omega-3 fatty acids found in fish can help with brain function and memory. Recent studies have found that people who ate tuna and other fish high in omega-3 fatty acids three times or more per week had a nearly 26% lower risk of memory related problems according to the journal *Neurology*. Omega-3 fatty acids are also available in supplements. Other amino acids, such as L-Tyrosine, as well as Thiamine, Niacin, and Vitamin B-6 have been shown to promote brain function and memory.

Foods containing antioxidants -- broccoli, blueberries, spinach, and berries, also promote healthy brain function. Some studies show that drinking at least 8 ounces of purple grape juice a day can improve your memory.

Grazing, or eating 5 or 6 small meals throughout the day instead of 3 large meals, also seems to improve mental functioning (including memory) by limiting dips in blood sugar, which may negatively affect the brain. Make sure it's healthy food selections, which brings us to another point.

Limiting the intake of food products containing estrogens can also be beneficial. In addition to the previous discussion of soy products, eliminating or minimizing the use of plastics containing BPA is also important. Water bottles, take out containers, baby bottles, and other temporary plastic containers should be lessened. These containers should never be used to reheat food or drinks, as the heating process leaches out more of the chemical. If possible, replace dairy and meat items with organic selections to lessen the amount of hormones injected through products where the animal has been fed antibiotics and hormones.

Hydration is also important to proper brain function. The brain and memory are not as effective if dehydrated. Caffeine can provide a temporary boost in energy and brain power, but if too much is in the system, it can lead to impaired performance, as can sugar.

Get Organized

Keep items that you frequently need, such as keys and eyeglasses, in the same place every time. Use an organizer or daily planner to keep track of appointments, due dates for bills, and other tasks. A simple notebook can work just as well as an expensive organizer. Keep phone numbers and addresses in an address book or enter them into your computer or cell phone. Improved organization can help free up your powers of concentration so that you can remember fewer routine things.

Eliminate / Minimize Stress

We live in a busy world where the majority of people do not take all of their vacation days each year in order to stay ahead at work, and those who work from home have been found to do to the equivalent of four fulltime jobs each week. Cortisol levels increase with greater amounts of stress and negatively impact memory function. While going off for a day a pampering or going on holiday may be out of the budget, committing to 10-15 minutes of mediation has been found to increase feelings of happiness, decrease stress, and encourage creativity. It can be a challenge to allow yourself to have even 10 minutes of quiet time each day, but meditation does not have to be a super power saved for a monk in a monastery high atop a hill. The process of sitting still and consciously turning off the little voice chattering in your head is meditation. A variety of websites offer guided meditations for free or a small fee if the task seems too daunting. Another option is to do a walking meditation, which is simply to get out and walk without the daily distractions (like phones).

Also, be sure to socialize. Studies have shown that both socialization and laughter improve memory. Even if friends are busy, take time to enjoy a funny show, film, or book to get a belly laugh and the brain engaged. Laughing also serves as an excellent way to increase the retention of new memories because the emotion tied to items is a pleasant experience.

Exercise

In line with the previous discussion of walking meditations, exercise raises endorphins in the blood, gets the blood pumping, and increases oxygen flow to the brain, among other benefits. Exercise does not have to be strenuous to see benefits. Walking briskly 3 times a week for 20 minutes is suitable. Studies have shown that even short amounts of activity like taking the stairs to work or parking further from the door can also benefit both mind and body.

Sleep

The amount of sleep we get affects the brain's ability to recall recently learned information. Harvard University studies indicate that getting a good night's sleep can improve the transitional memory between short-term and long-term memory. Though it is generally believed that seven hours is the necessary sleep time to function optimally, some studies acknowledge that individual sleep needs can vary from 6 to 10 hours a night.

While 10 hours of sleep each night may be a fantasy for those with busy lives, there are some ways to get better sleep. Go to bed and wake up at the same time every night and day. Don't try to "catch up" on sleep on the weekend. This has been proven as a false notion in sleep studies. Spend at least half an hour reading in bed and winding down before you go to bed. Shut off all electronics and items with blue spectrum light at least an hour before bed. Take power naps during the day, when possible. They can help you recharge your batteries and boost your memory. Limit the nap time to 20 minutes. Longer naps allow you to drop into deeper sleep and may actually cause you to wake feeling more tired if you awaken to an alarm.

Understand Your Attention Span

As you will recall, the opening section discussed the nature of "forgetting" things as a problem of registration, retention, or retrieval. Retention is directly linked to your attention span. The average attention span for an adult is 20-22 minutes. When engaged in a voluntary task that is of high interest that span can be increased to roughly 40 minutes. At that time, your brain needs a break to regain focus. Even in the case of watching a movie that is roughly 2 hours, you will notice that at certain points, whether in a theatre or are home, you will seem to get distracted for a few moments. You may look around the movie theatre or think about something else before refocusing on the film. This is the biological attention clock resetting.

To increase your retention, especially when dealing with written documents, you should plan to chunk your time for the greatest memory performance. Even while in social situations like a party, taking a break allows your brain to reset from sensory stimulation and process information for better storage, and later retrieval. When doing a task that requires memory and is more of a duty than a pleasure, breaks are even more critical for retention. In such cases, the goal should be to engage in the task for 20 minutes and then spend 10 minutes doing something else. If you are reading, engaging in a physical activity during the 10 minutes is the best option. It does not have to be intense exercise. Activities such as washing dishes, folding laundry, or simply walking around and getting a drink suffice. In social situations, changing locations and getting some "air" while looking at the view or your surroundings will allow your brain to reset without being antisocial.

Use Your Eyes

Studies show that moving your eyes from side to side for just 30 seconds once a day will align the two parts of your brain and make your memory work more smoothly. Try this trick when you wake up in the morning to help wake up your brain.

Aromatherapy

Studies show that smelling rosemary can improve your recall. Carry around a sprig of rosemary or smell rosemary oil once a day. The Ancient Greeks even put a sprig of rosemary behind their ears on exam days to help them boost their memories. Other memory boosters include basil, juniper berry, peppermint, sage or clary sage. While at home, the herbs can be placed in a small pot with water and simmered. Essential oils can be used in diffusers or combined with water in a spray bottle to mist the area and provide a brain boost.

Environmental Clues

Where using the loci method involved imagery and visualization, using environmental clues is about using your physical environment to aid your memory. To use environmental clues to remember something, you take an item and place it in an unusual location or position.

Example:

You need to remember to get a card for your parents' wedding anniversary.

You take a glass and place it in front of your door. When you go to leave the next morning, you will see the glass and it will trigger you to remember the anniversary before you leave in the morning. Another thing you could do is turn your coffee pot upside down. When you go to make your morning coffee, the fact the pot is upside down will trigger the memory as well.

Use Your Voice

When you need to remember something, do not simply rely on your thoughts. Use your voice to reinforce the item through physical and auditory pathways. As the saying goes, "We learn… 10 percent of what we read, 20 percent of what we hear, 30 percent of what we see, 50 percent of what we see and hear, 70 percent of what we discuss with others…" The reality is that mirroring back what you hear is also part of active listening. Not only does it reinforce what you are trying to remember, the person you repeat information back to is likely to feel validated for being heard correctly.

Example:

Your boss invited you to a lunch with a big client. You accept the invitation and close the conversation by saying, "Union Street Bistro, tomorrow at 11. I am looking forward to it."

Breathing

It helps to deepen your breathing when you have to remember something by breathing slower and deeper. Deeper and slower breathing actually changes the way your brain works, by causing the brain to switch to Theta waves. Theta waves normally occur in your brain in deep sleep. To activate your Theta waves, switch your breathing to your lower abdomen. Start breathing deeply from your stomach. Consciously slow your rate of breathing too. After a few moments, you should feel calmer with the Theta waves flowing in your brain; as a result you will be more receptive to remembering new information.

Marital Status

On an interesting side note, for these interested in brain and memory function later in life, an interesting new finding out of Sweden suggests that mid-life marital status is related to late-life cognitive function. The study of more than 1,400 people in mid-life and then an average of 21 years later showed that those who were living with a life partner in mid-life were significantly less likely to show memory decline compared to all other categories—single, separated, divorced or widowed. Granted, marriage may be stressful at times, but it appears that stress combined with the social aspect of relationships does promote a positive result in memory later in life.

Memory Tricks and Tips

With some of the background in brain and memory function covered, we shift to more of the practical ways in which you can improve your memory in every area of your life. Some of the tips and tricks are well documented to improve memory in brain research, while others are lesser known tools. You do not have to use every tip or trick covered to see your memory improve. After trying out a variety of tricks, most people find 2 or 3 that work best for them in a variety of situations.

Chunking

One of the mostly widely used memory tricks for remembering random items is chunking. Chunking utilizes the tendencies of the short term memory to remember a long list of items by breaking everything up into groups. Both the short term memory and long term memory work together to remember the individual groups as part of a larger whole list.

Example: Grocery Store List

Random List	Chunked List
Chicken	Chicken
Milk	
Bread	Milk
Yogurt	Yogurt
Cheese	Cheese
Crackers	
Bananas	Crackers
Broccoli	Cookies
Cookies	Bread
Onions	
	Bananas
	Onions
	Broccoli

Instead of trying to remember the random items on the shopping list, chunking the list into groups allows your brain to remember a few items in each category. The categories also correspond to the major areas of the market, which is part of the next memory trick, association.

Association

The grocery store list in the previous example used both chunking and association. The items were grouped into the areas of the market to make recall easier. Associations work by tying current information to previous information to make recall smoother.

Example:

Let's say you need to remember the combination to a lock, which is: 777122514.

You can begin by chunking the numbers in a way that is meaningful to you.

777 can stand for a jetliner

12, 25, and 14 can stand for Christmas day

You then associate the combination with a trip on Christmas day 777-12-25-14

Association also works well when meeting people. President Franklin D. Roosevelt used a technique for remembering peoples' names by imagining their name written on their forehead. This helps associate the name with the person in your brain. To take it a step further, learn an interesting fact about that person when you meet them and put an image of that fact along with the name.

Example:

You meet Jane and you find out she loves animals. You then associate a gorilla with her name on her forehead. Now you have associated not just the name and the interest to your new acquaintance, but you made a further association with Jane Goodall who is known for working with gorillas. The network of three associations will solidify her name in your memory.

Acronyms

Acronyms have been used for ages to remember items. Geography students learn about HOMES in relation to the Great Lakes as in Huron, Ontario, Michigan, Erie, and Superior. In math, students often are taught "FOIL" to remember how to multiply binomials as first, outer, inner last.

Acrostics

Acrostics are similar to acronyms, but instead of spelling out a word or name, the first letter of each item is part of a phrase. For example, learn the order of operations as "Please Excuse My Dear Aunt Sally", which is parenthesis, exponents, multiplication, division, addition, and subtraction. Music students learn very quickly that "Every Good Boy Does Fine" when memorizing the lines on the treble music staff.

Imagery

Another trick to remembering items that appear to be random is to create a mental picture or a story to go along with the items.

Example:

You need to get your coat from the dry cleaner, take your dog to the groomer, pay the light bill, and pick up flowers for your date that night.

You create a picture of you walking your dog at night with a flashlight and your date is at your side carrying a bouquet of flowers while wearing your jacket.

Another type of imagery memory trick is using loci to remember items. The loci method has been used since the time of the Greeks and is often referred to as the "Roman Room" technique. Instead of developing a picture of the items, you picture a room, house, or other building and locate all of the items in that space. As you travel in your mind around the space later, you collect the items that you aimed to remember.

You Try It: Roman Room - Here is your chance to practice the technique in real time. Below is a list of random items. Use them to create a room where you imagine all of the items before reviewing the example.

List of Words to Remember:

Pink roses

Baby grand piano

Mirror

Conch shell

Chess set

Dog

Hamster cage

Umbrella holder

Backpack

Vacuum

Airplane

Fried chicken

Shoes

Keys

Stamps

Purse

Fern

Ice cream

Example:

You walk into a living room with **pink roses** on the coffee table and a baby grand piano in the corner. There is a long **mirror** above the fireplace and on the mantle is a conch shell. A little boy sits on the couch playing with a chess set while a dog sleeps at his feet. A hamster in a ball travels across the room and the boy gets up to return him to the hamster cage near the door and next to an umbrella holder. The boy's **backpack** is open on the carpeted floor that needs a **vacuum**. The television screen shifts from a show about an airplane trip to a commercial about fried chicken. The boy's **shoes** are near the door where the mail lays waiting for **stamps** next to **keys** and a purse. A **fern** is on the other side of the door when a woman opens the door holding an **ice cream** cone.

Daily Practices

Believe it or not, aside from lifestyle changes that you may choose to make, your daily memory boosting practices involve playing games and solving puzzles. Engaging in a variety of games that involve strategy been proven to have positive effects on memory. There is a biological reward that comes from the release of dopamine when successfully completing games that boost the brain. Dopamine release is promoted by performing working memory tasks. Working memory tasks are truly biologically rewarding. A Swedish study took a selection of men in their twenties and trained them for 35 minutes per day for five weeks on working memory tasks with a difficulty level close to their personal limits. All subjects showed increased working memory capacity. Functional MRI scans showed that the memory training increased the density of areas in their cerebral cortex that are responsible for feelings of euphoria and reward. Yes, it is both productive and beneficial to your brain to play games.

Brain Games

A sequence of stimuli (pictures, shapes, numbers, letters, etc.) is presented. The classic n-back game or test consists of identifying when a current item matches one of the items a certain number of steps back. N equals the number of items back. It is similar to the classic game "Concentration". Instead of having cards in fixed locations on a table, there is a single item that appears in different locations on the screen. 1-N means that you need to recall the position of the previous item. 2-N requires the recollection of an item position 2 turns back, and so forth.

There are variations of the N-Back that have been popularized in recent brain game programs such as Luminosity, Cogmed,

MindSparke, and Jungle Memory. Such brain boosting and memory enhancing programs are designed to be used daily for less than 30 minutes. Some options allow the user to build on previous exercises, while other programs begin new exercises with each session. Interactive options for such brain games are available online and as mobile applications that are either free or for a charge. A Dual N Back Game is also available that increases the memory demand for further improvement of brain function.

Other strategy video games, such as the classic game Tetris, have been shown to greatly improve brain function and spatial recognition, while memory function is moderately improved.

Concentration

While the latest versions of the N-back game highlight the use of computers and technology, you can benefit equally with the classic Concentration game. You can play alone or with others and get the same benefits.

If you do not have the game, you can create your own version easily. All it takes is two decks of ordinary playing cards. Pair the two cards from each deck. Begin with 5 pairs of cards (10 cards total). The rationale for the grouping of 10 cards links to the capacity of the short term memory. When the 10 cards become easy to completely identify, add an additional set of 5 pairs. Eventually, you can work your way to matching 2 entire decks of cards (104 cards) if you practice enough.

Chess

To play chess well, you have to learn to expand working memory capacity to hold a plan for several offensive moves while at the same time holding a memory of how the opponent could respond to each of the moves. Not surprisingly there are studies showing that memory improves and IQ scores can go up after several months of chess playing. Chess has been proven to enhance memory due to the need to keep both offensive and defensive strategies in mind throughout the course of a chess match. Chess can be played as part of a social activity that further increases brain activity or as a solo endeavor using the traditional chessboard and playing both sides or using a computer, tablet, or smartphone. To increase the level of difficulty and test your memory skills, keep a game of chess going by only making 3 to 5 moves a day. When you return to the game, you brain and memory will be tested to pick up where you left off.

Other Puzzles

When brain games come to mind, the most recognizable options are the cognitive skills games such as the N-Back and chess, yet any type of puzzle activity improves brain function and memory skills. The popularity of Sudoku games is a testament to memory enhancement and challenge within the game format. The challenge is in remembering to think of the lines horizontally, vertically, and well as the sub-blocks within the larger puzzle. In this way, Sudoku can be seen as more difficult than chess and especially suited to solitary practice.

Crossword puzzles are beneficial for memory enhancement due to the requirement to decipher clues, recall facts, and fit material in a spatial plane. Brain games are not limited to numbers and letters, even the simple jigsaw puzzle can serve as a memory enhancer and a test of spatial recognition that fires connections throughout areas of the brain.

Playing Time

To realize the benefits of improved brain function and memory enhancement, the brain boosting games mentioned in this book should be performed for a minimum of 15-20 minutes a day, preferably every day. The aforementioned Swedish study regarding dopamine and the biological rewards for successfully engaging in these types of activities had participants performing tasks for 35 minutes, five days a week to see the measureable improvement. These exercises are not meant to be heavy lifting. They should be enjoyable. (After all, stress is bad for the memory too.) As long as you continue to enjoy the activity, you can participate in brain games for longer periods of time, but the minimum of 15-20 minutes a day should be maintained.

Quick List of Tactics for Boosting Your Brain Power

On the following pages, you will find a variety of tips, tricks, and information to enhance your memory. In some cases, the item reviews previous discussions. There are additional helpful items that did not get included in the general text. The quick list can be considered a "cheat sheet" for all of the material included in the book and is provided as a quick reference of material to implement for memory improvement.

1. Eliminate distractions and stop multitasking. Give your undivided attention to the task at hand to improve your ability to encode information and retrieve it at a later time.

2. Practice your memorization skills with a favorite song or poem. Work on memorizing a piece until you can say it to yourself without looking at the piece. Change the piece being memorized when you can recite it completely from memory. Do this regularly.

3. Use your creativity and other memory tricks to create a song or poem for items to be remembered.

4. Learn a language. You do not have to become fluent in a language to see improvement in your brain and memory. Learning simple vocabulary words is as effective as becoming fluent.

5. Learn to play an instrument. Reading, playing, and memorizing music is a memory boosting exercise that establishes connections across multiple areas of the brain that are responsible for memory.

6. Leave yourself a voicemail or email message to remind yourself about important tasks.

7. Write down events or tasks immediately.

If you don't have a pen to write something down immediately, use environmental clues as a reminder. If you always put your keys in your right pocket, put them in your left. If you wear rings or a watch, change the finger or wrist it is worn on.

8. Use a pen to make a mark on your hand. When you see the mark, it will trigger the memory of what you need to do.

9. When studying or reading, take a break every 20 minutes, and do something unrelated and physical. Then, go back to your task in 10 minutes.

10. Try a variety of brain boosting games to improve your memory.

11. To help remember names, look at the person when you are introduced and say the person's name: "Nice to meet you, Tom." If you know another person with the same name, picture the two holding hands.

12. Try yoga, stretching, or meditation to relieve stress. Remember to breathe deeply when trying to remember things.

13. Be sure to get sleep. When tired, try to fit in power naps of no more than 20 minutes to avoid feeling groggy rather than refreshed.

14. Use rosemary to help alert your brain to memory tasks. Carry a sprig or use essential oils.

15. Seek out humorous films, stories, and shows. Make it a point to laugh every day.

16. Check with a doctor or nutritionist for physical and nutritional components to a poor memory.

Stop saying that you have a bad memory. You are as you think. Celebrate the successes you have on the journey to a better memory.

Conclusion

The brain is the body's super computer, and memory is one of its major tasks. Improving your memory is a comprehensive process that encompasses all areas of life. The strictly mental tasks of encoding and retrieval are impacted by diverse factors such as physical and emotional well-being to nutrition. It is a common misconception that memory and intelligence are linked together and are fixed abilities. This is not the case. Memory is independent of intelligence, and both memory and intelligence can be enhanced through a variety of tricks, tips, and lifestyle choices.

By improving your overall health, you improve your brain function and memory. While memory is impacted by nutrition, stress, activity, and fatigue, and can be easily improved with different choices, it is important to be aware of more critical underlying concerns. If there is a sudden and rapid decline in memory and cognitive ability, it is essential to speak with a medical professional for screening of larger health concerns.

For those who are healthy, improving your memory can truly be approached as a fun exercise rather than a disconcerting effort. In addition to the various memory tips and tricks discussed throughout this book, brain function and memory performance are enhanced through games and tasks that engage the brain. As with the length of your attention span, the benefits of memory improvement activities will be enhanced by participating in activities that are personally enjoyable. You do not have to use every tip, trick, or practice exercise in this book to see improvement. By selecting the items that fit best within your schedule and interests, you will find that improving your memory is easy (and even fun) and can be done in minutes rather than in days, weeks, or months.

Your Free Gifts

As my way of saying thank for buying I put together two amazing free gifts for you.

These gifts are the ultimate bonus upgrade to this book…

The Brain Boosting Recipe Guide

&

The Sleep Hackers Quick Guide

To Download Visit:

www.GoodLivingPublishing.com/Brain

Thanks,

Andy Arnott

All rights Reserved. No part of this publication or the information in it may be quoted from or reproduced in any form by means such as printing, scanning, photocopying or otherwise without prior written permission of the copyright holder.

Disclaimer and Terms of Use: Effort has been made to ensure that the information in this book is accurate and complete, however, the author and the publisher do not warrant the accuracy of the information, text and graphics contained within the book due to the rapidly changing nature of science, research, known and unknown facts and internet. The Author and the publisher do not hold any responsibility for errors, omissions or contrary interpretation of the subject matter herein. This book is presented solely for motivational and informational purposes only.

Made in the USA
San Bernardino, CA
17 December 2018